DESERT MARIGOLD

DESERT MARIGOLD

POEMS BY

GODHULI C. GUPTA

Desert Marigold

ISBN: 979-8-218-20592-8

Book design & layout by Rachel Clift.
rcliftpoetry.com

First printing edition, 2023.

Godhuli C. Gupta
@wordsby.godhuli

A love note

Let me disrobe you
of your insecurities,
your heightened pretensions,
your illusions of such great expectations.
Let me kiss your anxieties away,
so you may no longer carry
the heavy burdens of the pretenses
you endlessly maintain.
Let me caress the gentle curves
of your body, serving everyone but your own.
Let me help you enter the cusp
of something beautiful,
something sacred,
for nothing else is as enticing
as the pure nakedness
of your *inner core.*

Table of Contents

Part I: The Yearning 1

Part II: The Birth 23

Part III: The Reclaiming. 43

Glossary. 65

Acknowledgments 67

Table of Contents

Part I: The Warning

Part II: The Birth

Part III: The Reclaiming

Glossary

Acknowledgments

Part I

The Yearning

Unbecoming

Is it too late to unbecome
the person I have become?

The good girl / the simpleton /
the poised professional / the silent
stereotype / the rule abider /
the dilettante / the people pleaser /
the passive participant /

The woman so paralyzed
by the fear of imperfecting
what's perfect.

Is it too late?

Sugar Cookie

You cut me like a sugar cookie,
molding me to perfection.
Saccharine sweet for every season—
stellar student, dutiful daughter
bashful bride, young mother.
I do not blame you for your ambitions,
but do you see how we crumble
under such great expectations?

The Mirror Doesn't Show

Why are we all
in a constant state of disguise,
I wonder out loud
as I stare into the mirror,
amused by all that you cannot see—
the wounds still nesting in a valley within,
the years of insecurity tucked safely away
in between cold bones,
the jealous rage that often erupts
in the darkest corners of my mind,
the heartaches that never fully healed.

The mirror doesn't show
what we don't want it to show,
so slowly we chip away
at each other's reflections,
longing for the walls to come down,
waiting to see the light within.

Young Girl

I saw you in the shadows
with the hesitation in your eyes,
and wish I could have told
you to not be afraid to take up
the space you so desired.
To stop *willing* the earth
to swallow you whole,
so you could crawl beneath
the surface and hide
beneath it all.

I salute you for your silent battles,
and see you for your desire to disappear,
but to minimize your magnificence
is an injustice. They *will* see you one day
for your intellect, your conviction,
the very *gravitas* of your presence.

You are safe, you are loved
and one by one, as we all sit up
a little taller, see how our shadows
manifest into one.

Finding their way,
toward the light.

Break the Cycle

She used to braid my hair and say
Darling, you are so lovely
but you need a little more
turmeric on your darkening skin,
a little more demure in your gaze,
softness in your stance, honey in your voice—
just a little more *practicality*
in your plans.

Is it really any wonder
that try as we may,
our natural inclination
is to acquiesce, avert our eyes
and bow down to the male gaze?

What you need now my love,
are ambitions beyond our comprehension,
conviction paired with confidence,
intellect over complexion,
and *dragons* in your eyes.

Bodies

I think often of all the young girls told
to cover up their bodies, before even knowing
what their bodies can do. Before being able
to spell or comprehend the word *shame.*

Do you know what it feels like to learn of desire
from the gaze of another? To be introduced
to something so beautiful and sublime,
under the shadow of a lion's pounce?

Can you feel the way it makes her shrink,
disappear, *loathe* the very thing that makes
her extraordinary? Shame simmers beneath
the surface, until it thickens into blank ink.

A slow suffocation.

I think often of these young girls, how
their bodies are held in captivity.
How they remain under the watchful
eye of everyone, but *their own.*

Dust

The word for melanin-rich
in my mother tongue is *dust*.

As if the bold coffee hues of our skin
somehow requires a deep cleanse
to better blend in with the complexion
of our colonizers.

As if the terracotta coating on our
soft rolling curves must be stripped
clean to better assimilate into
a certain purified aesthetic.

As if we can keep scrubbing and scrubbing
our bodies until it all dissipates—
the blood-soiled roots of our lineage,
the fervent song of our ancestors.

Until we are left with nothing
but the same skin, flesh and bones.

Where are you from?

after Riz Ahmed

How much time do you have?

Do you have time for me to tell you,
that I was born from the womb of a woman
torn away from her sanctuary to traverse
the seven seas, in pursuit of a dream
that was never entirely hers?

Do you have time for me to tell you
about the nation of my birth,
so devoted to preserving its own
ethnic purity, it could never offer
my brownness a home of its own?

My blood flows from a land so
ancient, yet nascent in its freedom.
Still aching from uprooting its
sons and daughters, mangled by
arbitrary lines of hateful division.

While my mouth spits flawless
English, my heart beats in Bengali,
and my soul reverberates with the
vigorous flame of the matriarchs
who prayed for my existence.

I can hum the morning *ragas*
of my mother's goddess worship,
sing rhymes alongside my children,
and sway with my husband to his
favorite soulful jazz.

Do you know what it's like?
To be neither here, neither there.
To fall in love, bring life into this world,
and pray for their acceptance—

Anywhere and everywhere.

Brown

You must be the nanny / do you go by any other name /
too pretty to be Indian / how is your English so flawless /
so thankful for your cultural expertise / but where are
you *really* from / how is your skin so light / I was hoping
you would say your earrings are from the streets of India /
so I can tell you about my spiritual experience in Varanasi /
what is the religious significance of / are you Hindi /
I'm cooking butter chicken today, isn't that grand / I'm dying
to visit / the colors are so vibrant / invite me to your
wedding / but can we wear real people clothes / so poised
and professional / stay silent and smile while I speak your
wisdom into the crowd / *this is my thank you for your presence
in this world.*

Belonging

Congratulations, she said kindly.

You are officially
the 'cultural ambassador'
of our class.

I look around the room,
the only brown woman
in a sea of future writers.

Thank you, I smile meekly,
accepting my award and
slinking to the back, trying
my hardest to *disappear*.

Magnificent Women

When will their stories be told,
the stories of the women we all know?
The ones who traveled across foreign seas,
trading in ambition for raising dynasties.

The bride who met her husband
on her wedding day, and promised
her daughters to never do the same,
silently grieving a life unlived.

The widow who toiled away
on her stove, only to eat her own meal
on the kitchen floor, basking in the laughter
of ten hungry little souls.

The young girl who crossed
blood-drenched borders, marching on
with hopeful pride, until she realized
the blood left behind.

What about all the women
whose martyrdom we casually praise,
without ever once questioning
their life's intent?

Why do we wait to tell their stories?
Mundane until it isn't,
magnificent when it's too late.

The Photograph

I have seen the photograph,
the one of my mother staring straight
at the camera, as if to say to her suitors
I dare you, pick me.

I can feel the fire simmering
beneath her eyes, all charcoal and grit,
aching for the air to release her
into the night.

Who was she
before fate swallowed her whole?

Before she was made to
carry my breath and my desires,
before the world chipped away
at the syntax of her soul?

Look a little closer.
Wipe away the dust and ashes,
be the breath

that ignites her *fire*.

Erased

I once had a classmate marvel at my flawless English,
as if mastering your accent was a finer accomplishment
than all the other languages under my belt.
No trace of your foreign origins, what an incredible feat.

I once had a neighbor with a suspicious stare,
who breathed a sigh of relief once he heard
the familiar blanket of a Western tongue.
Thank goodness, you're one of us too.

So we tell our little white lies
to put your minds at ease,
Don't apologize, it's my name that's difficult.
Our sons and our daughters
will be easier to pronounce.

While in our minds, we cannot forget what we felt
from our classmates, our neighbors, even our leaders,
that we do not belong unless we try to belong
& change & adjust & squeeze into your ideal
of what an American should look like, sound like, *smell like.*

These are the little poisons we hear and we say
that slowly erode our beautiful pasts.
How soon till our identities are completely *erased?*
How soon before it's too late?

Migrant

Sometimes I find myself
both drowning in the nostalgia
of makeshift homes swept away,
while grasping blindly
for lost connections.

When you live a life packed up in boxes,
transported to new lands oceans away,
pulled apart from friendly smiles
before you even knew what made them tick,
you wonder how you can ever commit.
You wonder how you can stop
the walls from closing in.

All I dream for us now
is a foundation rooted in
love and soil and time.

A love, without conditions.
A love, *without walls.*

Durga in the Diaspora

I have seen the pain in my parents' eyes
as they navigated the newness of their foreign homes,
tracking down local fish markets and spice stores,
gingerly knocking on the doors of social cliques,
unsure of whether they would ever welcome
our family of transient expats.

And yet something magical happened year after year
when the *dhak* beats of Durga Puja arrived,
my mother's *tanter* saris emerged from the suitcases,
my father donned his director's hat for cultural shows,
and my brother and I begrudgingly
performed alongside other nervous adolescents,
the *shine* finally returned in their eyes.

For these are the moments they waited for,
the feeling of finding community,
the thread that held us all together
in a quiet desperation to return
to the glory of our motherlands.

Ballerina in a Glass Box

I grew up as a ballerina in a glass box
Pristine, untouchable, unwavering
in my commitment to impress and delight,
a forever kind of performance.

My parents were so burdened by the need
to fit into a society they could never please,
prisoners to an image they
worked so hard to cultivate,
when simply *being* could have freed them
in so many monumental ways.

Having lived with their burdens,
my purpose is clear.
Shatter the glass box,
make way for unbridled ambition—
for how could I possibly let my children
be anything but *exactly*
who they are meant to be?

Good Girls

It starts so young
wild hair slicked back,
thighs covered & crossed,
whisper softly, good girls
don't cuss.

Until slowly it seeps into the depths
of your being and you find yourself
perfecting a demure, modest smile.

There's the steady unraveling and
ripening with age, the punching
realization of patriarchy in motion.

That as long as we keep our mouths shut,
legs closed, eyes down, they will continue
to suppress the wolves in our bones.

So stand tall, unleash the angst, let them
see the blood, snarl and baring teeth.
The world is on fire without
your fury and might.

Go show them
just how *good you can be.*

Part II

The Birth

Swan Song

She floated through life adorning masks
till motherhood ripped them off her flesh.
There is no time for act or pretense,
the stage lights are off
and the crowd awaits
to see what lies
beneath.

Growing

Why is it that I felt most free
when your bodies were growing inside of me?
My darling babies, you gave me permission
for the roundness in my belly,
the dimples on my thighs,
the stripes on my torso,
the fullness in my cheeks.

I could finally let out a deep exhale
and just let my body *be*.

Abandonment Issues

Live your life with abandon, they say
Until it's time for children,
whom you obviously cannot abandon.
But if you do, make sure it's for ambition,
which you must also never abandon,
because if you do, it's a surefire way
to abandon your sense of self.
And when it comes
to what you really need,
they say *I will never abandon you.*
Until they all do
over and over again.

Why Can't You?

Follow your calling, they say.
Do not let motherhood
erase your identity.

In between the hourly cat naps,
the round the clock feedings,
the piles of clothes on your bed,
the pungent odor of breast milk on your shirt,
the constant desire to be rocked,
the mid-morning pump
before your breasts explode,
the dire emotional state
of your firstborn.

How dare you let yourself go?
And let down generations
of women before you.

Unseen

How do you make your presence
felt when the only tabs in your mind
consist of schedules, lists, and the
mundanities of everyday life?

When the conversations you carry
are full of empty lies and the varnished
truths of a seemingly perfect life?
How do you make yourself feel
just a *little less* invisible when suddenly
you find it difficult to quantify
your contributions,
your very existence?

Check in on the mothers
who smile sweetly and claim
they are fine, while inside they tremble
with the realization
of *what could have been.*

We were once magnanimous
creatures of substance,
drunk on ambitions
now abandoned.

A Woman's Worth

Most days I walk around
with breast milk stains on my overnight shirt,
flyaway baby hairs eclipsing my gaze,
tired sullen skin begging for a cleanse,
a reflection in the mirror
I can barely stand,

And I wonder how you could possibly
still love the golden girl you fell for.
The woman who used to dance on bars,
show off her legs, and light up the room
with her big brown eyes.

I wonder how much you really mean it
when you tell me what I'm worth.
But despite my hesitation, I beg you
to never stop reminding me
of what I'm really worth.

Bedtime

Just one more.

One more storybook
One more stuffed animal
One more hug
One more sip of water
One more cuddle
One more diaper change
One more gummy vitamin
One more *piercing shriek*
One more tickle.

Heads exploding,
spirits breaking,
backs aching.

One more final kiss and we slink away,
collapsing on our couch, flipping wordlessly
through their pictures on our phones.

When We Can Breathe Again

Good morning
You take her, I'll take him
Take her to the park to visit the swans
Let her run wild to her little heart's content
I'll take him and his insatiable hunger,
rocking him to sleep hour after hour.

Good afternoon
Let her eat well, nap well, play well
Brush her little curls the way she desires
I'll take him and his insatiable hunger,
rocking him to sleep hour after hour.

Good night
You take bath time, I'll take lullabies
Somewhere in between,
Can we steal a quick kiss?
Under the weight of promises kept,
we whisper to each other—

I'll see you when we can breathe again.

Love is Not Anger

The thing about anger is
that it leaves little holes throughout
your body, begging to be filled
with love and affection.

And when you repeatedly
endure it in what you believe
to be your sanctuary,
you begin to associate love
with the fiery passion of a flame
that licks away at your core.

You will learn in time
that love is steady and even
a little mundane, with no
blazing fire in sight.
That it simmers gently
and patiently with
the delicate radiance
of swirling incense.

The Motherhood Club

Once you're in,
they'll tell you it's all a farce
and slowly peel back
the layers of anxiety, anguish
and endless self-doubt.
To say it's all worth it
is stating the obvious.
Give me instead
the raw, honest
universal truths
that make us feel less
like floating stars in an endless galaxy.
All it takes is a single voice
to say, *I feel this too.*
But till then may you continue to revel
in the picture-perfect parts of it all
because isn't it magical,
this ride we call *motherhood.*

Envy

Is it strange that I am often jealous of you?
Jealous of your purity, your confidence,
your spunk, your innate goofiness,
your ability to make everyone fall in love
with you so seamlessly.

I pray that this world never robs
you of these qualities, and that you
remain brazen and bold,
for your mother gave up long ago.

Room For Two

Everyone tells you how your love
will multiply to make room for two,
but no one tells you
how much your heart will ache
when you lose your firstborn to the village
that swallows her whole in a show of
extraordinary, unconditional love
as you plough through the ugly newborn days
and pick up your shattered little pieces.

No one will tell you
how much your heart will ache
when you notice how much her lashes have grown,
how her dainty little face has matured,
and how sad her eyes look
when she begs for a few extra minutes
on the bedroom floor.

Nothing can prepare you
for the heartache,
yet somehow your beautiful broken heart
makes *room for two.*

Legacy

What traces of culture
will I impart on her soul?

Will the sound of soft *ghazals*
provide the same sense of calm?
Will the sight of *dhak* players
put a smile on her face,
will the taste of fresh coconuts
make her tongue come alive,
will the scent of incense
inspire a moment of reflection,

but most important of them all—
will she learn to let love in
with wide open arms?

What legacy will we leave behind,
before they leave us all behind?

Voices of our Ancestors

At night, I hear the voices
of our ancestors taunting me.
I feel the vermilion from my forehead
clawing into my skin. The silver *payals*
which once adorned my ankles so delicately
now weighing heavily on my feet.

As if to say, *you are not worthy of our sacrifices.*
Not good enough to mother.

What once felt like the shiny allure
of tradition now feels like taut rope,
tethering me to a version of myself
that no longer looks or feels like me.
Who am I to light a fire on the bricks
laid out for me? Who am I to redefine
the proper way to *mother?*

But listen more closely to the voices
of our matriarchs. Hear the pain
in their whispers. Let them show you
the sliver of light at the door.

All you can do is open it.
Let the light in.

Mourning the Mother Tongue

When I find myself mourning
my mother tongue, these are
the things I hold onto—

The way my daughter marvels
at her reflection in her iridescent
lehenga, tenderly caressing her
dupatta like an heirloom jewel.

The way my son sits still
on his grandmother's lap,
mesmerized by the harmonious
flow of her morning prayers.

The way their eyes light up
when little idioms slip from
our native tongues, as if they've
found a favorite old song.

The way slow-simmered
chicken curry will always serve
as a soft balm for all the madness
in this world.

The way love, in the
absence of language,
always transcends.

Never lost in translation.

For the First-Time Mother

You will love / you will mourn / you will resent /
you will get down on your knees and pray / you will
self-destruct / you will doubt / you will rage / you will
walk / you will sway / you will wish for them to see you /
you will inhale [their entire existence into yours] / you will
crumble / you will beg for the unsolicited advice / you will
wish people just stopped sharing how their babies slept
through the night / you will listen / you will reject / you
will bleed / you will writhe in pain / you will wonder if
desire will ever return / till slowly you rise / you will find
the light / you will conquer / you will discover your
knowing / and yes, you will love.

Oh, how madly you will love.

Good Mothers

Stop the glorification
of the good mother /
the sacrificial mother /
the tireless mother /
the mother who surrenders
body, mind and soul
out of societal expectation—
homemade dinners on the table every night,
seasonal arts and crafts,
kitschy traditions for festive weekends,
even a momentary pause on marital bliss.

Instead raise up the mothers
who choose wisely to nourish their souls,
pick self-love over perfection,
and destroy the notion
that pouring endlessly from parts unknown
is what defines a *good mother.*

Part III

The Reclaiming

Endless Infinities

Somewhere in this cosmic chaos,
I stole a moment for myself.
Drinking in the summer breeze,
hypnotized by the ombre swirls
of God's masterpiece.
And somewhere in the velvet sky,
she came back to me—
the woman I used to be,
home to *endless infinities.*

The vows we should have exchanged

Some days it will be difficult for you to love me.
I'll be hiding in our closet, clutching my insecurities
in the palm of my hands, willing you to soothe me
with fire in my eyes and tears clouding my judgment.

Some days it will be hard for you to look at me.
I'll be bent over in bone-crushing pain,
spilling my insides out, screaming words
I can't return into thin air.

Some days I'll learn that the silence in the air
is not a lack of empathy, but an inability to express
what's in your soul. And that sometimes I express
myself a little too much, too often, too loudly.

Some days the simple act of bringing me coffee
or watching you kiss our children can overwhelm
me beyond belief.

And every Sunday morning I'm lucky enough
to wake up next to you, I'll hold back tears of gratitude.

For the way *you carry me, the way I carry you.*

A Moment

There is this beautiful moment
right before I drift off to sleep
when I truly believe I have all that I need.

A moment when comparison
is no longer the thief of joy,
a moment when self-doubt ceases to exist,
and envy stops rearing its ugly head.

A moment when only my softest,
most delicate and pure instincts remain
and I can feel the rhythm of your breath,
and the gentle whispers of their tender sleep
humming deep inside of me.

If only I could carry this moment
into all my days,
how perfect my days
would be.

Home

I do not want a home
curated to perfection,
styled by the design goddesses
of the Internet.

Give me a home that is instead
a living, breathing reflection
of our beautiful mess—
toys strewn across the couch,
the vintage Persian rugs
with wine stains from last night,
Ma Kalis and Durgas adorning
our white walls, and mismatched
collectibles from trips
around the world.

Give me the bold vibrancy
of our beautiful culture,
the sound of sweet *ghazals*
wafting through the kitchen,
traces of turmeric on shiny white
countertops, and your favorite blues
humming in the basement.

Give me Sunday mornings
with hot coffee, your sweet breath,
and their tiny arms
wrapped around my neck.

May Our Daughters

May our daughters shine with their lustrous
skin, delicately kissed by the sepia soil
of our motherland. Eyes like midnight,
burning arrows into our souls.

May our daughters leave tremors
wherever they go, with legs of might
and hips so rapturous they drip
with caramel sweetness.

May our daughters emerge from the shadows.
Let down their velvet hair, flaunt a mind
of their own. A voice that *conquers*
instead of being conquered.

May our daughters finally see
how good it feels to bask in the light.
To *luxuriate* in all its glory.

Stretch

Wake up,
open your eyes.

Take another look at yourself
Caress the flashes of silver on your torso
See how they *flow* like tiny streams
towards an ocean of possibility.
How they twirl like intricate vines
ascending to the heavens.
Adorning the valleys of your skin,
like nature's permanent kiss.

Don't you see?
These are the scars of a feline
poised to pounce.
The shedding of one life
to another. The battle wounds
of a warrior queen.

Take another look,
honor the evolution.
See just how far
you can rise.

Scent of a Sari

There's nothing quite like
the scent of my mother's sari
wrapped up in the thickness
of my childhood nostalgia
of perfume, elegance, and tranquility.

I grew up in between the folds of her sari,
caressing my cheeks against its soft fabric,
basking in the safety of its sweet musk.

I still sneak into her closet at times,
running my fingers through threads
from every corner of the world—
dhakai, tant, silk, baluchari, benarasi.

Each time entranced by their power
to transform her into an ethereal being.
I close my eyes and breathe it all in—
for I have found my sanctuary, at last.

About My Name

You once asked me about my name,
but how do I explain the complexity of a name
curated so thoughtfully from ancient Sanskrit
script, from a father working tirelessly abroad,
heart aching for the familiar old song.

I could tell you I once saw my name
on a cocktail menu in Calcutta—what is foreign
and strange to one man is another man's elixir.
Can you taste the honey in your mouth?

Do you feel the weight of history and poetry,
see the cattle dust and bleeding rust,
the lustrous flight of colors as they settle
into the sky for yet another evening of slumber?

I could tell you all these things, but my name
crumbles like chalk. Too delicate to touch,
like *powder* on your tongue.

Cultured

To the girls who once ridiculed
the coconut oil glistening
in my raven hair,
I see your turmeric lattes,
your *Ayurvedic* potions,
your cries for body positivity.
How dare you made me once feel
like I was anything
but a goddess.

Ancient Indian Beauty Secrets That Will Make You Look Great

Tell us, what is the significance of
the heirloom jewels that grace
your mother's anklets? Tell us
something delightful and quirky
about its heritage, but not the part
about us stealing them as our
seasonal accessory of choice.

Tell us what turmeric & sandalwood
can do for my aging complexion,
but kindly look away when I turn
your secrets into my millions.

Tell us how it feels, when your
voices slip away from the telling
of your stories.

When the conquest never ends.

Daughters

I do not believe in reincarnation
but sometimes when I catch
the glimmer in your eyes,
and the carefree manner
with which you toss your hair
and sway your hips, I do believe
you were sent to me from my past,
to show me what life could look like
had I been set fully free—

to show me a life with wings.

Sons

To the sons
who tumbled out of wombs
dripping with amber sweetness
and warm embraces, may the world
never strip you of your softness.
May you continue to flow through
life with your tender touch and
endless capacity for joy, rejecting
the notion that to be a man in this
world you must wear steel armors
and walls for emotions. May you
lean into a definition of manhood
that intertwines vulnerability,
empathy and love to create the most
impenetrable strength, the same
way spider silk is so delicately
woven to weather every storm.

Aflame

Whatever it is
that sets your soul aflame,
chase it.

Let down your hair and dance
with your ancestors in goddess worship.
Wear the dress with the low-cut back
and the earrings that graze your neck.
Sway with the lady at your favorite blues bar,
the one with the voice of a smooth
cappuccino. Then scream with rage
into the belly of the night.

Forever is too delicate
an illusion to live life
without fire.

My God Resides Within Me

My God resides within me,
tucked away in a deep exhale after a long day,
resting in the depth of my love's kiss,
dancing in the glisten of my daughter's eyes.

My God makes her presence felt
in the lips that soothe my son's fears,
in the fire that fuels my ambition,
and in the tenderness of my tears.

My God, she is unfazed and unbound
by the weight of your opinions,
and the judgment cast by your glare.

My God resides within me—for me,
in a place that is simple and pure,
where strength and vulnerability
can peacefully coincide.

Tapestry

Every part of my body
is an atlas of all the lives
I have lived. Trace your fingers
from top to bottom and feel
the laugh lines,
the rivers of wisdom
etched into my smile,
the softness of my curves
overflowing with joy.

Try as you may,
you cannot erase
the depth of my living.
The very tapestry
of my being.

The New Anthem for Brown Daughters

You are the untamed tempest
of a midsummer evening,
brazen against rose-colored skies.

You are the gold dust shimmer
from sun's eternal worship,
lighting your melanin on fire.

You are one with the wind,
like the luscious locks of your crown,
drinking from the nectar of our gods.

You are both Kali and Durga,
entangled in fury and might.
unbothered by man's delight.

You are nobody but yourself,
so go on and surrender—
give in to *desire.*

Desert Marigold

She rose like a sea
of desert marigolds
blooming against all odds.
Intertwined in solidarity,
resplendent under
the brazen sun.

Beautiful creatures,
how they take time to bloom.
But once they do,
see how they set
the entire desert aflame
with their electric
orange hues.

Glossary

"Where You From": A spoken word piece by award-winning British-Pakistani actor & rapper Riz Ahmed for the film *The Long Goodbye.*

> *"Maybe I'm from everywhere and nowhere*
> *No man's land, between the trenches."*

Raga: A melodic framework for improvisations and composition in classical Indian music. Each raga lends itself to a different mood, season, or time of day.

Dhak: A large, cylindrical-shaped drum popular in the West Bengal region of India. Played with two thin wooden sticks to create an upbeat, celebratory sound integral to Hindu religious festivals like Durga Puja.

Goddess Durga: In Hinduism, Goddess Durga is the protective mother of the universe. She is one of the principal forms of Shakti, the divine female energy. Durga is the warrior goddess of protection, strength and motherhood. Commonly depicted with ten arms, a third eye, riding a lion and slaying Mahishashura, the evil buffalo demon.

Durga Puja: An annual ten-day Hindu festival celebrating Goddess Durga's destruction & victory over evil. The festival is extremely popular among the Bengali diaspora around the world—a community-building event and social celebration.

Sari: A large, unstitched piece of fabric draped intricately over a woman's body. The ultimate mark of classic style & sophistication in South Asian fashion. Types of saris include:

- *Dhakai:* A light cotton sari hailing from the Bangladeshi capital of Dhaka.
- *Tant or tanter:* A traditional sari from West Bengal, woven from light cotton threads for hot summer months.
- *Baluchari:* A type of Bengali silk sari known for its

intricate depiction of mythological scenes on its borders.

- *Benarasi:* A beautifully made sari from the Varanasi region of India. Made of finely woven silk with intricate and opulent embroidery and engravings.

These are just a few types of saris featured in the poem 'Scent of a Sari.' There are many different types of saris spanning the various regions of South Asia.

Lehenga: A traditional ankle length skirt paired with a blouse and *dupatta*, usually worn for festivals and weddings.

Dupatta: A long, shawl-like scarf traditionally worn by South Asian women to cover their head or drape over their shoulders.

Payal: Anklet.

Ma Kali: "The Dark Mother," Ma Kali is the goddess of power, time, destruction, and fertility. She emerged from Goddess Durga to destroy evil and defend the innocent. Kali is popularly worshipped in West Bengal as a benevolent mother who protects her devotees and children from misfortune.

Ghazals: Short, poetic verses originating from Arab poetry. They were popularized in South Asia in the Urdu language, and tend to be romantic in nature.

Sanskrit: The ancient, sacred language of Hinduism.

Ayurvedic: A system of medicine originating in India more than 3,000 years ago. 'Ayurveda' literally translates to 'knowledge of life' and focuses on herbal remedies and natural, holistic techniques.

Acknowledgements

We Didn't Have

We didn't have 'I love yous'
We had cut up fruits as afternoon snacks,
nightly oil massages and yogurt face masks,
a box full of mangoes at summer's first kiss.

We didn't have 'I'm so proud of yous'
We had framed art projects on full display,
celebratory sweets for every occasion,
and a myriad of rituals to ward off the evil eye.

We didn't have 'I'll be there for yous'
But somehow they always were,
across borders and time zones,
diplomas and grandkids, there they were—
preparing containers full of curries,
burning the midnight oil.

To my parents—what I can't express in simple words, I express through poetry. Thank you will never be enough.

To my husband & darling babies—for being my muses and infusing my work with so much purpose & meaning. I wrote this book for you.

To my brother—for being my first call, my first read, my creative partner in crime. We're on this journey together.

To Rachel Clift—for this beautiful cover, this beautiful book. For guiding me through this exhilarating journey of self-publication.

To Leslie Yeary—for the kindness in your heart and for editing my collection with so much thought & selflessness.

About the Author

Godhuli Chatterjee Gupta is a first-generation South Asian American writer and poet. She is a former "third culture kid" who has grown up in six countries around the world and currently resides in the suburbs of Chicago raising her two children with her husband.

Godhuli attributes her love of poetry to her Bengali immigrant parents, who immersed her childhood with art, theater, film, and culture. Her colorful upbringing gives her a unique perspective on identity, language, borders, family, and relationships.

Godhuli has a bachelor's degree in Journalism and a master's degree in Integrated Marketing Communications from Northwestern University.

Website: wordsbygodhuli.com
Instagram: @wordsby.godhuli

9 798218 205928

Printed by Libri Plureos GmbH in Hamburg,
Germany